MAIN LINE STEAM AROUND LONDON

THE PRESERVATION YEARS SINCE 1968

MALCOLM BATTEN

AMBERLEY

First published 2021

Amberley Publishing
The Hill, Stroud
Gloucestershire, GL5 4EP

www.amberley-books.com

ISBN 978 1 3981 0101 2 (print)
ISBN 978 1 3981 0102 9 (ebook)

British Library Cataloguing in Publication Data.
A catalogue record for this book is available from the British Library.

Typesetting by SJmagic DESIGN SERVICES, India.
Printed in the UK.

Introduction

On 11 August 1968 BR bade farewell to standard-gauge steam with the famous 'Fifteen Guinea Special', and it was all over. A steam ban was placed barring all steam trains from running over BR metals. The only exception was the privately preserved LNER A3 Pacific No. 4472 *Flying Scotsman* for which owner Alan Peglar had negotiated a deal allowing it to run on BR until 1972. However, in 1969 he took the engine to the USA for a government-backed tour promoting British goods and travel. He then chose to embark on a second USA tour in 1970 without sponsorship, but this proved disastrous and bankrupted him. A rescue operation bankrolled by William McAlpine brought *Flying Scotsman* back to England in 1972.

The main line steam ban was soon to come to an end. In October 1971 GWR King Class 6000 *King George V* passed through Kensington Olympia with the Bulmers Cider Pullman coaches as part of an eight-day trial tour. A list of approved routes for steam-hauled excursion trains was drawn up. This was to comprise less busy provincial lines, where any such operations were less likely to disrupt normal traffic. London, with its busy main line and commuter traffic, was not included! So, the only opportunity to see a working steam locomotive in London was to come at the occasional open days held at railway depots. In fact, a very early opportunity came with an open day at Cricklewood Depot in July 1969. To ride behind steam, you would have needed to visit one of the few fledgling preserved lines and heritage centres that were beginning to open, although the nearest of these to London were the Bluebell Railway in Sussex or the Didcot Railway Centre in Oxfordshire.

Gradually, the routes available to working steam were extended. Then on 1 March 1979 *King George V* hauled a special train from London Paddington to Didcot to commemorate the 125th anniversary of the opening of Paddington. On 20 September 1981 BR 9F 92220 *Evening Star* and GWR 'Castle' 5051 *Drysllwyn Castle* top-and-tailed a shuttle from Paddington to an Old Oak Common depot open day.

While these were one-off events, there were steam-hauled tours that started from London with diesel or electric haulage from the capital. For instance, in June 1983 there were three workings of 'The Shakespeare Express' from Paddington with steam haulage from Didcot to Stratford-on-Avon.

But the main breakthrough year was 1985, for it was then that regular steam excursions began running from Marylebone to Stratford-on-Avon. The Post Office was planning a 'Famous Trains' stamp issue for January 1985 and wanted a loco in steam for the official launch. As A4 Class No. 4498 *Sir Nigel Gresley* was the only locomotive depicted on the stamps to be preserved, this was chosen for the occasion. The line out of Marylebone had been proposed for closure and running the train into Marylebone was seen as something of a morale booster. Furthermore, the line was relatively quiet – Marylebone station was often used for film work with steam locos (though not in steam) and it had a working turntable. No. 4498 worked its passage to Marylebone with the 'Thames-Avon Pullman' from Saltley, Birmingham, on 12 January to become the first engine to run *into* London on railtour duty in the post-1968 era. This would not be the first visit by No. 4498 to the station – it had been named there in 1937.

The Post Office launch was carried out on 21 January, after which tourists and visitors could ride to Lord's Tunnel and back behind No. 4498 for 50p.

After the success of this venture BR gave approval for a Sunday round trip to Stratford-on-Avon to test the market. The first 'Thames-Avon Express' ran on 26 January and proved highly popular. This later became the regular 'Shakespeare Limited'. A range of different locomotives were brought in to work this and the various enthusiast charters that also ran over the route. Locomotives from all four pre-nationalisation companies had a chance to show their paces over the next three years plus BR built 4-6-0 75069. But the star of the show was undoubtedly the NRM's record-breaking *Mallard* restored to running order, which worked three 'Shakespeare Limited' trains. However, all good things come to an end, and with engineering work possessions and the resignalling of the Marylebone line scheduled, the regular steam workings finished at the end of 1988, although some enthusiast tours continued thereafter.

1985 was also the 150th anniversary of the founding of the Great Western Railway, so a number of events were held to commemorate this, including an open day at Old Oak Common Depot at which *King George V* and a replica broad-gauge *Iron Duke* each gave rides along a length of track.

Other routes from London followed, but the Southern Region lines fitted with third rail electrification were to remain barred. Concerns over lineside trespass by members of the public on other routes on the occasions when steam had been allowed to run since the early 1970s was the reason for this. Some station rail shows were held at Southern Region stations where locomotives were in static steam, but these locomotives were going nowhere – there were even sleepers chained across the tracks to emphasise this! This situation was not to be lifted until 1992, and initially steam running was only after dark. However, once the all-clear had been given in 1994, it has been the lines from Victoria and Waterloo that have witnessed more steam workings from London than any of the other routes. This has partly been because the network of routes allows for several circular routeings, thus not requiring another locomotive on the rear of the train to release the stock on arrival at the destination. The Venice Simplon-Orient Express Pullman stock began to be steam hauled in 1994 after *Clan Line* was fitted with air brake equipment to be compatible with the stock. This still runs but is now marketed as the 'Belmond British Pullman'.

Privatisation from 1994 opened up new opportunities as Railtrack had an 'open access' policy and was unable to impose the same rules on main line steam operation as BR had done. Amongst the new innovations in 1994 was the first steam working out of Kings Cross since 1969, and this despite the route now having overhead 25 kV electrification.

Various companies were formed or expanded to tap into the growing market of steam trips from London. Hertfordshire Rail Tours, already well known for organising diesel-hauled tours, branched into steam tours in the 1990s and ran some trips utilising rebuilt 'Merchant Navy' No. 35028 *Clan Line*.

The Railway Touring Company, based at King's Lynn, was founded in 1997 and continues to offer not only day trips and rail holidays in the UK, but also in Europe and worldwide.

The Mid-Hants Railway, which has a main line connection at Alton, set up a venture called Daylight Railtours in 1998 to run steam trips with their main line-certificated locomotives from the railway to locations on the main line network, often passing through London on the way. One of their most ambitious ventures was the 'Alresford Adventurer' on 11 November 2001, which started at Alresford station on the Mid-Hants, came up to and around London to eventually reach Walton-on-the-Naze, Essex, passing through the other Alresford station on the line from Colchester. On the return journey, after a reversal at Colchester Town, the train proceeded up the Sudbury branch with a stop at the East Anglian Railway Museum at Chappel

& Wakes Colne. The original date had to be put back a week owing to engineering works, and in the meantime British Summer Time had ended, so it got dark earlier. I joined this train in London and we lost time en route through engineering slacks and operational difficulties so that we were over an hour late and in darkness when we reached Chappel. The Railway Museum there had had to stay open after their normal closing time to await our arrival. I don't know what time the train eventually made it back to the Mid-Hants but it must have been a very long day for the crews and on-train staff. The locomotive was No. 35005 *Canadian Pacific*.

One of the main players in organising steam-hauled excursions, Steam Dreams, was founded by Marcus Robertson in 1999. On Thursday 16 December, BR Standard 5 4-6-0 No. 73096, based on the Mid-Hants Railway, departed from Waterloo at 11.00 a.m. with the *Wessex Belle*, routed via the main line to Woking and on to Salisbury. This was a test run to prove that steam could operate successfully alongside the busy schedule of electric trains with their faster acceleration and permitted line speeds. Arrival in Salisbury was just two minutes down and the trip was judged a success, leading to the establishment of a programme of excursions the following year. Steam Dreams are based near Guildford, Surrey, and so developed initially around their home market. Their original concept was the 'Cathedrals Express' circular tour running to Canterbury or Salisbury on a format of three hours there, three hours stay, and three hours back. Locomotives and stock were initially provided by the Mid-Hants Railway using the same resources as for their own Daylight Railtours, which ceased in 2004.

Following the initial success of this, their programme became increasingly ambitious each year. In the 2002 season programme they had trips from London to Canterbury, Chichester, Portsmouth, Winchester, Salisbury, Bath, Bristol, Ely and Norwich, all on circular routings. They also featured pre-Christmas excursions including carol concerts at cathedrals, and this has since become an annual part of the programme. Not all Steam Dreams trips now start from London – there are a number that start from outer suburban locations and cross London en route or avoid the London area altogether. There are also now railway-based holiday tours such as the 'Cathedrals Explorer' and 'Highlands & Islands Explorer' holidays and since 2015 also 'Emerald Isle Express' holidays running in Ireland.

Crews and rolling stock for many of the steam-hauled tours run by Steam Dreams and other tour operators are now provided by the West Coast Railway Company. They run out of the former Southall loco depot that had been operated as a heritage steam centre beforehand by the GWR Preservation Group. This had been acquired by a consortium of steam operators to create a London base after operations ceased at Marylebone Depot. The 'Belmond British Pullman' however operates out of Stewarts Lane Depot and the stock is also regularly used with diesel haulage provided by DB Schenker.

Now under the chairmanship of locomotive owner David Buck, a new venture for Steam Dreams in 2019 was the 'Royal Windsor Steam Express' running three trips a day every Tuesday from 4 June until 3 September between London Waterloo and Windsor & Eton Riverside. Passengers travelled outwards by steam, returning to London by normal service trains. In addition, there was an evening 'Sunset Steam Express' dining train. Results of the season's operation show that almost 10,000 passengers were carried throughout, way above the original estimate, and that many of the passengers were younger people who had not previously patronised steam trips. The evening dining train was sold out in advance for the final six weeks it ran. It is intended that the Windsor trains will be expanded for the 2020 season and new destinations sought for similar programmes.

It is nearly fifty years since the main line steam ban was lifted in 1971. Since then, the country's railway network has seen varying fortunes, from continued run-down and line closures in the 1970s, privatisation, and revival. Despite several scares that various legislation (for example, health and safety, emissions, etc.) might limit or ban heritage steam on the main line, and varying attitudes from rail company managers and government transport ministers towards its presence, steam excursions have continued to prosper and now there are main line steam excursions from London almost every week throughout the year.

Unfortunately the programme of steam operations in 2020, like other 'non-essential' activities, was suspended as the coronavirus epidemic swept through the country and lockdowns were imposed. Steam Dreams and other operators 2020 programmes were wiped out. The lockdowns have continued into 2021 with a gradual staged lifting of restrictions and it is only from mid-May 2021 that services have been able to resume.

All photographs are by the author except where stated.

Photographers should note that not all the locations featured in this book remain suitable for use today. Some lines have since been electrified. Footbridges have been meshed in, replaced or just removed. On some main lines out of London, such as the Great Eastern and Great Western, the main line tracks have been fenced off from the suburban lines to prevent would-be suicides. At least, with the majority of services being on the Southern third rail network, overhead electrification masts and wires are not a problem on these lines.

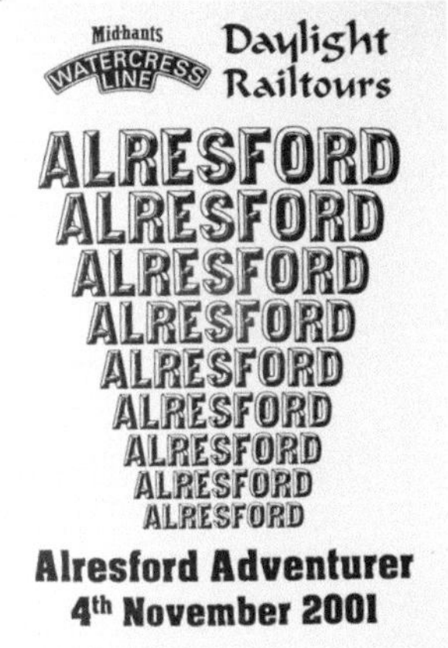

Flashback

The predecessor to today's enthusiast steam specials can be traced back to 1938. It was then that the LNER brought the ex-Great Northern Railway 1870 single-wheeler No. 1 out of the original York museum and restored it to working order to haul a train of vintage carriages from London to Stevenage as part of a press launch on 30 June for the new rolling stock being introduced on to the 'Flying Scotsman' service. Later the Railway Correspondence & Travel Society chartered the engine and coaches for a trip to Peterborough on Sunday 11 September. The RCTS special is seen near St Neots on its way to Peterborough. (Photo by Reg Batten)

On 1 May 1968, shortly before the end of BR steam, A3 No. 4472 *Flying Scotsman* bursts out of Hadley Wood tunnel on the day of its epic non-stop run from Kings Cross to Edinburgh, forty years to the day since the first non-stop run. A second tender had been purchased in 1966 to carry water because of the removal of water troughs and columns. (Photo by Reg Batten)

1969–84: Early Days

A rare early opportunity to see preserved steam locomotives in steam came when an open day was held at Cricklewood Depot on 12 July 1969. One of the locomotives present there was GWR Castle Class 4-6-0 No. 7029 *Clun Castle*.

Also at the Cricklewood open day was ex-LMS 'Jubilee' 4-6-0 No. 5593 *Kolhapur*, one of four of the class to survive.

In 1979, the NRM's replica of Stephenson's *Rocket* was exhibited in steam on a length of track by the Albert Memorial in London's Kensington Gardens, Hyde Park. This was in connection with the 150th anniversary of the Liverpool & Manchester Railway. This photograph was taken on 26 August. On 10 March 1980 the *Rocket* replica also appeared in steam at St Pancras to publicise a GPO stamp issue.

On 1 March 1979 No. 6000 *King George V* departs from Paddington with the special train to commemorate 125 years of the opening of Paddington, paced by one of its modern successors, a Class 43 HST. The *King* failed on arrival at Didcot and the return train was diesel-hauled. (Photo by Geoff Silcock)

On 20 September 1981 an open day was held at Old Oak Common Depot to mark the 75th anniversary of the depot. A shuttle service from Paddington was worked with BR 9F 92220 *Evening Star* and GWR 'Castle' 5051 *Drysllwyn Castle* top-and-tailed. The 9F is seen approaching Old Oak Common. The Grand Union Canal lies beyond the wall behind the train. (Photo by Geoff Silcock)

A 'Britannia' returns to Stratford! The doyen of the class was the star guest at an open day held at Stratford TMD on 9 July 1983. When the class was first introduced in 1951 the first examples were used on London–Norwich expresses and would have been based and serviced at Stratford Depot. (Photo by Reg Batten)

A new station building was provided at North Woolwich on the branch line from Stratford in 1979. The Grade II listed former station building became the North Woolwich Old Station Museum in 1984. This was formally opened by HM The Queen Mother on 20 November, who arrived by train, hauled from Stratford by none other than *Flying Scotsman*! A test/gauging run was made the previous day and 4472 is seen here near Stratford Market on that occasion. The locomotive was serviced at Stratford TMD, who characteristically gave it a white-painted cab roof for the duration. (Photo by Geoff Silcock)

1985–93: The Return of Regular Steam from Marylebone

A major feature of 1985 was the celebrations to mark 150 years of the Great Western Railway. A replica of the Great Western Railway 1847-built, broad-gauge 4-2-2 *Iron Duke* was built by Resco (Railways) Ltd of Woolwich and the tender and two carriages constructed by BR at Cardiff. This was first steamed on display in Kensington Gardens in April 1985 and was photographed on 8 April.

The GWR *Iron Duke* replica ran with the replica coaches on a length of track installed at the Old Oak Common Depot open day held on 15 September 1985 as part of the 150 years celebrations.

Also giving rides at Old Oak Common was 6000 *King George V*. The bell was presented when the locomotive visited America in 1927 for the centenary of the Baltimore & Ohio Railroad. LMS Pacific 46229 *Duchess of Hamilton* was on static display along with Prairie tank No. 5572 from Didcot.

1985 was the year when regular steam-hauled excursions began from Marylebone to Stratford-on-Avon. Ex LMS 'Coronation' Class Pacific 46229 *Duchess of Hamilton* departs from Marylebone with the 'Shakespeare Limited' train on 21 July 1985. This had arrived in London on 4 May on the 'South Yorkshireman' charter from Sheffield.

Locomotives for the services were stabled at the Marylebone DMU cleaning shed, and lighting up and coaling was carried out in the milk dock between the depot and the main line. Facilities were basic and coaling was largely reliant on muscle power or mechanical grabs as arranged by the support crews. A diesel shunter was allocated to Marylebone to shunt dead locomotives. BR Class 4 4-6-0 75069 was awaiting attention on this occasion. This only ran briefly during March–April 1986. (Photo by Reg Batten)

Ex-LNER A4 Pacific 4498 *Sir Nigel Gresley* heads the 'Shakespeare Limited' approaching Willesden Green, 15 June 1986. The London Underground Jubilee and Metropolitan line tracks are to the left. This was owned by the A4 Locomotive Society and was based at Carnforth before coming to London to initiate the excursions from Marylebone in 1985.

Preserved as part of the National Collection, A4 4468 *Mallard* was returned to steam in 1986 to celebrate the fiftieth anniversary of its world speed record, and worked some of the trains from Marylebone including three additional trips on the 'Shakespeare Limited' as here passing Ruislip Gardens on 26 October 1986.

An open day held at Cannon Street station on 23/24 August 1986 featured 'King Arthur' 777 *Sir Lamiel* amongst the exhibits. Note the sleeper chained to the track ahead of it – this loco was going nowhere! Note also the 'Southern' style 'Shakespeare Limited' headboard. Also part of the National Collection, this worked on the Marylebone tours between April 1986 and June 1987.

No. 4472 *Flying Scotsman* heads the 'Shakespeare Limited' at Willesden Green on 22 March 1987. Coupled behind the loco is one of the dreaded 'ETHELS' (Electric Train Heating Ex-Locomotive), No. 97252 *Ethel 3*. These were created from Class 25 diesel locomotives to provide electric train heating to the coaches as it was considered too costly to maintain steam heating equipment on the coaches.

Rebuilt 'Merchant Navy' Pacific 35028 *Clan Line* passing Neasden on 11 October 1987. Once again 97252 *Ethel 3* is in use. *Clan Line* had been the second locomotive to work into Marylebone on a charter on 2 March 1985, ready to work its first train to Stratford-on-Avon on 30 March. Owned by the Merchant Navy Locomotive Preservation Society, *Clan Line* was bought out of service in 1967 as being the last of its class to receive a major repair and a boiler regarded as in the best condition.

In the pre-Christmas period of 1986 and 1987 some 'Santa's Steam Special' trains were run between Marylebone and High Wycombe and proved very successful. On 12 December 1987 'Black 5' No. 5305 *Alderman A. E. Draper* was in charge. Being December, 97252 *Ethel 3* was also in the formation. The train was photographed at Sudbury & Harrow Road.

On 17 October 1987 an open day was held at the Ripple Lane Depot, Dagenham. Amongst the exhibits were two steam locomotives supplied from the Midland Railway Centre at Butterley. One of these was LMS Stainer 8F 2-8-0 48151. Remarkably this event went ahead only a few days after the Great Storm of 1987, at a time when some parts of the national network were still cut off as a result of storm damage.

The other locomotive was BR Standard 2-6-4T No. 80080, a locomotive that had started its career when new on the London, Tilbury & Southend line and so would have regularly passed through Dagenham. The two locomotives ran under their own power with a support coach to and from London via the Chiltern line.

Un-rebuilt Bulleid Pacific 34092 *City of Wells* passes through Sudbury & Harrow Road with the 'Shakespeare Limited' on 12 June 1988. This was the first Bulleid Pacific to be rescued from Barry scrapyard in 1971 and was restored by 1979. Fitted with a Giesl ejector, this was a loco that could be relied upon to provide plenty of 'clag'! However, the locomotive was retired from main line work later in 1988 when its seven-year BR boiler certificate expired.

Not all the steam workings on the Chiltern line originated from Marylebone. On 2 October 1988 GWR 'Castle' 7029 *Clun Castle* from the Birmingham Railway Museum at Tyseley worked 'The Inter-City' train from there to London and back. Here it approaches Neasden on the inward journey.

On another occasion in 1988 7029 *Clun Castle* is seen again passing through West Ruislip. (Photo by Reg Batten)

On 9 May 1988 No. 4468 *Mallard* was employed to haul 'The Postal Pullman' charter to Banbury for a Royal Mail stamp launch which featured the locomotive on the first-class stamp to commemorate 150 years of the Travelling Post Office. It was seen approaching Willesden Green with the mail coaches at the head of the train.

An open day exhibition was held at Waterloo station on 1 October 1988. 35028 *Clan Line* was at the end of a platform – a location it must have stood at many times during its working life. Note the sleeper placed ahead of it, although at least this time it is not chained in place!

Also on display at Waterloo was M7 0-4-4T No. 245 from the National Railway Museum. These locomotives were long associated with empty stock workings to/from Waterloo.

'Black 5' 44932 was displayed at Richmond on 8 December 1989. This was as a preview to a rail show at Windsor & Eton Riverside on 10 December where 44932 was also on display.

Rebuilt Bulleid Pacific No. 34027 *Taw Valley* was an exhibit at an open day held at London Bridge station 31 March 1991. On 7 June 1992 this would become the first steam locomotive post-1968 to run over the third rail when it ran into here after working a series of Ashford–Hastings shuttles (on a line not electrified). 34027 was first steamed in preservation in 1987 and then saw regular main line use until 2001.

Left: 35028 *Clan Line* featured at the Wimbledon TMD open day held on 6 May 1991 where it gave rides within the depot boundaries. The third rail was of course turned off for the duration.

Below: 5029 *Nunney Castle* with a 'William Shakespeare' railtour from Paddington nears West Ealing on 31 May 1992. On 9 December 1991 this had hauled the first steam train out of Paddington since 92220 *Evening Star* and 5051 *Drysllwyn Castle* top-and-tailed back in 1981.

1994–99: Privatisation and Steam Back on Electrified Tracks

Bulleid rebuilt 'West Country' Pacific 34027 *Taw Valley* passes Raynes Park with the 'South Western Swansong' on 19 February 1994. Departing Waterloo at 9.00 a.m., this was the first daylight departure by steam from here since 1967. It was also timed to the new 75 mph speed limit – steam had previously been limited to 60 mph on the main line.

LMS Stanier Pacific 46203 *Princess Margaret Rose* with the 'Inter City' approaching West Drayton on 26 March 1994. This ran to Didcot and was the first stage of five legs run to mark the end of the BR InterCity brand with privatisation. These would culminate in a series of workings between Crewe and Holyhead. This is one of two of the class to survive, the other being 46201 *Princess Elizabeth*.

The first BR Standard Pacific 70000 *Britannia* carries the 'Golden Arrow' headboard, arrows and flags as it passes Sydenham Hill on 7 May 1994. It is also running in the guise of a long-lost classmate – No. 70014 *Iron Duke* – a practice later enacted by other locomotives as we shall see elsewhere. The train ran to Folkestone Central as part of the celebrations marking the opening of the Channel Tunnel.

Gresley A4 Pacific 60009 *Union of South Africa* worked 'The Elizabethan' tour out of Kings Cross on 29 October 1994. This was the first steam working out of Kings Cross since *Flying Scotsman* in August 1969 and commemorated thirty years since 60009 hauled the last BR steam train out of the terminus in 1964. The train ran to Peterborough under the overhead wires. As this was sold out, a repeat run ran on the next day. This was routed via the Hertford loop and is seen at Palmers Green.

LMS Pacific 46229 *Duchess of Hamilton*, also at West Drayton but this time on the fast line, on 6 November 1994 with a 'William Shakespeare' working to Stratford-on-Avon via Didcot and Oxford.

The first three weekends of December 1994 saw a series of 'Santa Steam Specials' – four trips per day – on a circular working mainly over Southern metals from Kensington Olympia. Two Severn Valley Railway-based locomotives were used. Ivatt Class 2MT 46521 heads away from Willesden Junction (high level) towards Acton Wells on 4 December 1994.

46521 approaches the 'Jacobs Ladder' footbridge at West Ealing with stock from the 4 December Santa workings.

46521 again, between Chiswick and Barnes Bridge on 4 December 1994.

The other locomotive used on the 'Santa Steam Specials' was BR 4MT 2-6-4T 80079 which is seen paused in Chiswick station on 11 December 1994.

80079 again, crossing Barnes Bridge on 18 December 1994.

Having come off the North London line at South Acton, 80079 waits in the loop at Kew Bridge to join the Southern route through Chiswick and Putney and back to Kensington Olympia on 17 December 1994.

After Christmas the same locomotives were used on 'Mince Pie Specials' circular tours out of Paddington. These ran out and back via the Greenford loop on 27–28 December. 46521 bursts out of the tunnel section from Drayton Green and enters Castle Bar Park, 27 December 1994.

80079 passes through Castle Bar Park station in the opposite direction around the Greenford loop on 27 December 1994. The two engines then returned north with 'The Severn Cotswoldsman' tour from Paddington to Kidderminster on 1 January, replacing the scheduled 5029 *Nunney Castle*.

60009 *Union of South Africa* heads down the South-Western main line at New Malden on 18 February 1995 with an excursion to Exeter. Owned by Scottish farmer and landowner John Cameron since withdrawal in 1966, until 1984 this locomotive only ran in Scotland, but since then has travelled all over the country.

6024 *King Edward I* approaches West Ealing at 'Jacobs Ladder' with 'The Red Dragon' from Swansea to Paddington running on the fast lines on 1 March 1995. This was the '*King's*' final run before its boiler ticket expired.

'The Woking Centenarian' ran on 24 March 1995. Arranged by Woking Council as part of the celebrations of the borough's centenary, this featured No. 35028 *Clan Line* leaving Woking at 06.35 a.m. and running into Waterloo during the morning rush hour. The train is seen passing New Malden. A return working left Waterloo at 19.09 p.m. Season ticket holders could pay a £4 supplement to ride the train. During the day *Clan Line* worked a schools' special from Woking to Salisbury and back.

The unique LMS 'Black Five' fitted with Stephensons link motion rather than the normal Walschaerts valve gear, 44767 *George Stephenson* waits for departure time from St Pancras with 'The Mancunian' on 22 April 1995. This had arrived at St Pancras in March with 'Days Out's' 'The Palatine' from Stockport – the first steam working into St Pancras since 1962 except for the replica *Rocket* in 1980.

35028 *Clan Line* passes Vauxhall on 11 June 1995 with LSW Railtours' first 'The Strong Countryman' tour to Bournemouth and back. This was a reference to the lineside signs formerly erected by the brewers Strong & Co. of Romsey featuring steam trains and stating 'You are approaching (or you are in) the Strong Country'. Despite the rainy conditions here, later in 1995, the entire national steam programme would be cancelled from 30 June to 16 September because of the fire risk in a summer of drought conditions.

'Merchant Navy' Pacific 35028 *Clan Line* is running as long-lost classmate 35017 *Belgian Marine* as it passes South Croydon with the VSOE Orient Express Pullman stock on 19 April 1996. *Clan Line* was fitted with air brake equipment on overhaul in 1988, the first steam locomotive to be so fitted in the preservation era. This enabled it to work the air brake-fitted VSOE Pullman stock, which it did for the first time in September 1994.

35028 *Clan Line* nears Stoats Nest Junction, at the site of the former Coulsdon North station, 23 May 1997. This has continued to be the main steam locomotive on the VSOE Pullman workings. The popular Surrey Hills lunchtime circular dining tours from Victoria via Guildford began in 1996.

35028 *Clan Line* enters Coulsdon South on 21 November 1997. The lunchtime VSOE circulars via Guildford were originally routed outwards via Croydon and Redhill, returning via Staines.

35028 *Clan Line* approaches Putney on the return leg, 4 April 1997.

35028 *Clan Line* passes Earls Court on 15 December 1996. The exhibition centre has since been demolished. To the right at lower level are the District line tracks from Earls Court to Olympia. The headboard recalls the former 'Ocean Liner Specials' that ran from Waterloo to Southampton Docks to convey passengers to and from the great liners. During the year the locomotive was used on boat trains to Southampton Docks in connection with sailings by the *Queen Elizabeth 2* and *Oriana*.

Southern Railway S15 Class 4-6-0 No. 828 was bought from Barry scrapyard by the Eastleigh Railway Preservation Society and moved to Eastleigh works in March 1981. Restoration was completed in 1993. Here it is seen at Sutton on 11 February 1996. The 'Southern Vanguard' train had started from Portsmouth Harbour and included photographic run-pasts on the Horsham–Dorking line.

S15 828 has steam to spare as it runs through West Drayton on the fast line towards London Paddington with the LSW Railtours Southampton–Kensington Olympia–Clapham Junction train on 9 November 1996. The S15 was now carrying the nameplates *Harry A. Frith* after the former Eastleigh erecting shop foreman who supervised its restoration.

34027 *Taw Valley* takes the curve through Crystal Palace on 8 December 1997. The VSOE lunchtime circulars were routed via Crystal Palace to East Croydon rather than along the busier main line route through Norbiton. Like *Clan Line*, *Taw Valley* has been fitted with air brakes.

A rear view as 35028 *Clan Line* passes through Kensington Olympia on the centre road with the VSOE stock on 5 November 1997

'Black 5' 44767 *George Stephenson* passes New Malden on 31 January 1998. It was paired with Class 33 D6593, probably to provide train heating.

Steam trains from Victoria normally depart from platform 2. However, on 12 May 1998 a different platform was used for some reason, and so we see *Clan Line* not departing from platform 2 but being photographed from there.

Purchased from Barry scrapyard in 1980, The Mid-Hants Railway's U Class 2-6-0 No. 31625 was restored to main line running standards and made some trips on the main line between 1997–99. Here it approaches Syon Lane on the Hounslow loop with the 'West London Explorer' on 9 January 1999.

U Class 31625 waits to depart Waterloo with 'The Capital Explorer' on 30 January 1999. In 1999 this also participated in London Underground's 'Steam on the Met' specials.

The prototype Gresley V2 2-6-2 *Green Arrow* is preserved as part of the National Railway Museum collection. On 14 March 1999 it passes through Sudbury & Harrow Road with an excursion from Marylebone. An overhaul paid for by a private sponsor saw the locomotive repainted in BR green livery as No. 60800 during 1998.

BR 4MT 2-6-4Ts 80079 and 80098 had worked down to London on 1 May 1999 with 'The London Standard' which was routed over the Bedford–Bletchley line. On 2 and 3 May they would work three trips between Fenchurch Street and Southend Central. On 2 May 80098 brings the empty stock to form the train through Stratford to reach Fenchurch Street via Bow Junction.

80079 is on the rear of the train as it passes through Stratford station.

After a visit to Australia in 1988–89, and then a period operating on heritage lines as it did not have a main line certificate, Gresley A3 'Pacific' 4472 *Flying Scotsman* returned to the main line after overhaul in 1999. It was now with its third owner, Tony Marchington, and the paint was still wet when it attracted the attention of the public and media on its inaugural return trip at Kings Cross 4 July 1999. Note the piper on the extreme right. This was the first visit by the engine to Kings Cross since 31 August 1969, its last trip before being shipped to America. *Flying Scotsman* now had a non-authentic pairing of a double chimney, A4 boiler and LNER green livery.

2000–08: Enter Steam Dreams

BR Class 5 4-6-0 73096 is another locomotive based on the Mid-Hants Railway that was restored to main line standards. On 16 December 1999 it worked 'The Wessex Belle', which is seen passing through Raynes Park. This was a test run to prove that steam could operate successfully alongside the busy schedule of electric trains with their faster acceleration and permitted line speeds. This paved the way for Steam Dreams operations to start in 2000. No. 73096 was painted in BR green livery rather than the customary lined black because it had been allocated to the Western Region at Shrewsbury and the WR tended to paint all passenger engines green whatever the BR guidelines might be!

34016 the 'Cathedrals Express' trains to Canterbury began in 2000 and were routed from Victoria to Bromley South via the Catford loop. On 23 August 2000 34016 *Bodmin* takes the Catford loop curve at Nunhead that will bring it out to join the main line through Bromley South at Shortlands.

34016 *Bodmin* passes through Crofton Park on the Catford loop line on 9 August 2000. This Mid-Hants-based engine had gained a main line certificate after an overhaul was completed in June 2000.

Bodmin is well into its stride as it leaves the outskirts of Greater London and heads into Kent approaching Swanley station on 15 August 2001.

Ivatt 2MT 2-6-2T 41312 from the Mid-Hants Railway at Staines on 26 March 2000 with 'The March Hare'. It ran trips between Staines and Windsor & Eton Riverside.

41312 crosses the River Thames as it departs from Windsor, 26 March 2000.

41312 awaits departure at Windsor & Eton Riverside, 26 March 2000.

Rebuilt 'Merchant Navy' Pacific 35005 *Canadian Pacific* waits to depart from Waterloo on 16 August 2001. Only the Eurostar platform buildings in the background mar a scene that could have been from the 1960s.

35005 *Canadian Pacific* waits for a signal check at Wanstead Park station on the Gospel Oak to Barking line on 11 November 2001. This was the on 'Alresford Adventurer' railtour, starting from the Mid-Hants Railway and diverted from the North London line because of engineering works. It would proceed to Woodgrange Park, where the diesel on the rear of the train would bring it back over the link at Forest Gate Junction to reach the Great Eastern main line. It then picked up passengers (myself included) at Forest Gate in lieu of Stratford before heading for Colchester and Walton-on-the-Naze.

A pre-Christmas 'Cathedrals Express' to Ely saw 35005 routed through Edmonton Green on 5 December 2001.

Steam workings in or out of Paddington tended to use platform 1 on the far left of the station. 7029 *Clun Castle* has arrived here with 'The Capital Castle' on 19 May 2001 and makes a contrast with the HSTs that were their current successors on the GWR main line.

BR 4MT 2-6-0 76079 passes Pudding Mill Lane on 7 May 2001 with a departure from Liverpool Street.

Ian Riley's 'Black 5' 45407 in the guise of 45157 *The Lancashire Fusilier* runs through Stratford with 'The Norfolkman', 5 May 2001.

BR Class 4 2-6-0 76079 passes Harold Wood on 4 May 2002 with a 'Cockney Coaster' trip returning from Southend Victoria.

Crisp winter sunlight glints off B1 No. 61264 as it passes White Hart Lane on 9 November 2002. One of two Thompson B1s preserved, 61264 was the only ex-LNER locomotive to pass to Woodham Bros scrapyard at Barry from whence it was bought. Restoration was completed at Loughborough in 1997.

A4 60009 *Union of South Africa* gets a turn on the Surrey Hills lunchtime circular via Guildford with the VSOE stock passing Barnes on 14 March 2003. These trains had been amended to run outwards via Staines and back through Redhill and East Croydon, rather than the other way round as was originally the case.

The driver of BR Class 5 4-6-0 No. 73096 takes his train gingerly over the Ealing–Greenford line approaching South Greenford on 30 April 2003. There were severe speed restrictions on this section of the line at the time, probably due to subsidence of the bank.

73096 makes an impressive sight as it storms through Denmark Hill with a 'Cathedrals Express' on 23 July 2003. Let's hope the locals didn't complain about the pollution!

An LMS Pacific on its home turf. No. 6201 *Princess Elizabeth* with 'The Merseyside Express' at North Wembley on 4 July 2003.

No. 4472 *Flying Scotsman* was signed up for the VSOE Pullman workings from London Victoria. Here it is passing Barnes on 14 November 2003. German-style smoke deflectors had now been fitted, making it even more unauthentic when painted in LNER livery.

Looking quite at home and in period with its lined BR black livery and maroon Mark 1 coaches, B1 4-6-0 61264 passes through Manor Park with 'The Broadsman' tour to Norwich and Lowestoft on 10 April 2004. Unfortunately, on this occasion, the locomotive hit the buffers at Norwich during a run-round procedure and Network Rail then impounded the B1 on allegations that the brakes were faulty.

Another former Barry scrapyard engine, Bulleid Pacific No. 34067 *Tangmere* returned to steam in 2003. Operated by its then owner under the Wessex Trains banner, the locomotive subsequently passed to Ian Riley and then to West Coast Railways. Here it passes Coulsdon on 7 May 2004.

34067 *Tangmere* at Clapham Junction cutting on 1 July 2004. The inevitable graffiti 'adorns' the cutting wall.

Carrying the full 'Golden Arrow' regalia, *Tangmere* makes a spirited departure south from Kensington Olympia on 18 July 2004. It had taken over the train here.

GWR 'King' 6024 *King Edward I* heads for Paddington past West Drayton on 11 December 2004.

A pre-Christmas 'Cathedrals Express' on 17 December 2005 saw 'Black 5' No. 45321 *The Sherwood Forester* routed unusually via Mitcham Junction.

No. 45231 *The Sherwood Forester* passes through Denmark Hill station on 7 June 2006.

No. 45231 awaits departure at Waterloo platform 19 on 12 December 2006. This platform, alongside the former Eurostar platforms, is the longest at Waterloo and is the usual preference for steam workings from the station.

No. 6233 *Duchess of Sutherland* is seen on arrival at Kings Cross on 29 October 2006.

Later in the afternoon, No. 6233 waits at Harringay with the empty stock, which it will haul over the connection on to the North London line and onwards to Southall for servicing, 29 October 2006.

The NRM's V2 4771 *Green Arrow* was repainted back into LNER green in 2006. Here it nears journey's end to London at New Southgate on 18 November 2006. Unfortunately, the V2 is now a static exhibit as the monobloc cylinder casting was showing signs of wear and replacement would be too expensive to consider.

An excursion to Marylebone on 1 April 2006 was top-and-tailed with 8F No. 48151 leading. This was seen passing Sudbury & Harrow Road.

'Jubilee' Class No. 5690 *Leander* was on the rear of the same train, 1 April 2006.

Also photographed at Sudbury & Harrow Road is GWR 'Hall' Class 4965 *Rood Ashton Hall* from Tyseley. This was taken on 5 May 2007.

Southern Railway No. 850 *Lord Nelson*, the doyen of its class, was selected for official preservation as part of the National collection. Restoration to main line working order was completed at Carnforth in 1980. However, boiler problems led to it being static for many years and it was not until another overhaul paid for by a Heritage Lottery Fund application that the locomotive returned to the main line in 2007 and returned to London. It passes Shortlands on 16 May 2007. Boiler problems persisted and *Lord Nelson* was consigned to the Mid-Hants Railway.

The sole example built of a BR 8P Pacific, No. 71000 *Duke of Gloucester* heads westwards at Iver on 6 April 2007 with the first leg of 'The Great Britain' holiday tour.

No. 34067 *Tangmere* makes a fine sight speeding through Raynes Park on the main line tracks. With the green-painted support coach to the fore, this could almost be a scene from the 1960s (except for that modern high-intensity light on the front of course). 12 September 2007.

Another fine sight as No. 34067 crosses Richmond bridge in low winter sunshine, 20 December 2007.

We saw No. 6233 *Duchess of Sutherland* on the East Coast Main Line earlier in October 2006. It was back again a year later and its picture taken passing New Southgate on 6 October 2007.

Duchess of Sutherland had a spell on the 'Cathedrals Express' workings in 2008 and was seen passing through Brixton on 30 July. Note the fine headboard.

In May 2007 LNER A4 No. 60019 *Bittern* returned to steam at the Mid-Hants Railway for the first time since 1973. Its first main line trip was from Kings Cross to York on 1 December. Here it approaches Barnes Bridge on 16 July 2008.

A rear view frames 70013 *Oliver Cromwell* with the signal as it speeds through Raynes Park on 14 September 2008.

2009 Onwards: New Variety, New Liveries, New Locations and a New-build

New-build Peppercorn A1 Class 4-6-2 No. 60163 *Tornado* passes New Southgate on 7 February 2009. This was the first run into London by the £3m new-build locomotive, unveiled in 2008. The journey was from Darlington, and crowds thronged the platforms at Kings Cross to photograph it on arrival.

A 'Britannia' back at Liverpool Street! No. 70013 *Oliver Cromwell* has arrived with 'The Easterling' from Norwich on 16 May 2009.

On 25 July 2009 60019 *Bittern* made the 188-mile run from Kings Cross to York non-stop utilising two corridor tenders. This enabled not only sufficient water to be carried but also a crew change en route, just as in the former days of the 'Elizabethan', etc. The train is seen passing Harringay. The 'Brighton Belle' headboard seems somewhat incongruous!

Crisp, low winter sunshine illuminates 35028 *Clan Line* as it crosses the Thames at Chelsea with the Pullman stock on 19 December 2009.

A side-on view of *Clan Line* as it crosses the bridge. A pier in the foreground and high-rise developments on the south bank have spoilt this location since.

No. 6201 *Princess Elizabeth* and the empty stock of its train are drawn into the carriage sidings at Clapham Junction for servicing. Later in the day the train would return north via Kensington Olympia. 6 March 2010

'Castle' Class 5043 *Earl of Mount Edgcumbe* passes Hanwell on the morning of Saturday 17 April 2010. This was part of the GWR 175 celebrations.

Later in the morning No. 5043 heads over Hanwell viaduct on the fast lines with a non-stop train to Bristol. The first full brake coach contains additional water tanks to avoid the need for a water stop. The following day No. 5043 returned to Tyseley via Oxford.

The NRM's 'King Arthur' *Sir Lamiel* received BR Brunswick green livery on overhaul in 1989. Now as No. 30777 it passes through Peckham Rye on the 'Cathedrals Express' on 29 April 2010.

No. 30777 *Sir Lamiel* near Iver on 23 April 2010. The locomotive was withdrawn from main line use in 2013, as it was increasingly found to be out of gauge for many routes. The bridge here was later demolished without replacement and the line now has overhead electrification.

70013 *Oliver Cromwell* passes Barnes on May Bank Holiday Monday 3 May 2010. This was on one of four trips between Victoria and Windsor & Eton Riverside for the Girl Guides Association. The morning trips had steam haulage to Windsor and diesel back to London, in the afternoon (as here) the opposite situation applied.

New-build A1 60163 *Tornado* worked over a wide range of the national network in its first few years. Here it heads out east from Liverpool Street and passes through Manor Park on 28 May 2010.

A1 60163 *Tornado* heads out with the VSOE Pullman stock at Kew Bridge, 20 August 2010.

60163 *Tornado* passes through Wandsworth Common on the return journey to Victoria on 20 August 2010.

A4 60019 *Bittern* departs from Chiswick on 25 August 2010 with the 'Dorset Coast Express' which was booked to pick up passengers here. I narrowly missed losing this photo as the London-bound EMU just pulled into the platform as *Bittern* departed!

No such problem with 'Black 5' No. 44932 at Chiswick on the 'Dorset Coast Express' on 1 September 2010.

44932 again, approaching Chiswick with a 'Cathedrals Express' and seen from the Great Chertsey Road bridge, 5 August 2010.

44932 was out again on 11 August with another 'Cathedrals Express' working. This time it is heading down the Brighton main line towards East Croydon and is seen in the cutting between Clapham Junction and Wandsworth Common.

Not all steam tours have been organised by traditional railtour operating companies. The Faversham-based brewers Shepherd Neame organised a series of annual tours from London around Kent and visiting Faversham for the Hop Festival and tours of their brewery, reliving the days of the 'Hop Pickers Specials'. Some of these tours also included trips up the branch from Sittingbourne to Sheerness. On 5 September 2010 No. 44932 approaches Gravesend with the 'Spitfire' tour (named after one of their main ales).

During the winter of 2010–11 A4 *Bittern* was refitted with the valences it had earlier carried when masquerading as No. 2509 *Silver Link* and was repainted in LNER garter blue with the identity of No. 4492 *Dominion of New Zealand*. Here it is seen at Kings Cross on 16 April 2011 with both tenders in use. The length of the train with both tenders made a front view impossible.

No. 4492 heads north at New Southgate on 4 June 2011 with the 'Cathedrals Express'. Only one tender was in use on this occasion.

No. 4492 again, approaching Putney on 26 July 2011 and both tenders are in use. As can be seen the second tender is just for water. The London Underground District line to Wimbledon crosses the line by the arched bridge under which the train is passing.

On 24 April 2011 'Castle' Class No. 5029 *Nunney Castle* worked the final leg of the 'Great Britain' up to London. Later in the day 5029 and the stock were turned using the Greenford loop. Here it passes Drayton Green.

Steam Dreams ran the 'Cathedrals Explorer' from 6 May 2011. 'Black 5' 45305 worked the first leg from Kent to Victoria, and is seen nearing journey's end at Wandsworth Road.

The train was taken forward from Victoria by 6201 *Princess Elizabeth* which is entering West Brompton, 6 May 2011.

A GWR loco on the West Coast Main Line. Tyseley's 'Castle' Class No. 5043 *Earl of Mount Edgcumbe* drifts through Carpenders Park as it approaches Euston on 21 May 2011.

No. 70000 *Britannia* heads north from Kings Cross at Oakleigh Park on 21 August 2011. This had been repainted in unlined BR black at this time.

No. 70000 *Britannia* comes off the Barking–Gospel Oak line at Gospel Oak to join the North London line, 31 August 2011.

No. 70000 *Britannia* crosses the River Lea at South Tottenham on 10 December 2011, again on the Barking–Gospel Oak line. The train had started from Southend Central.

A1 60163 *Tornado* runs through an unusually deserted Peckham Rye station on 18 June 2011. This had now been painted in BR Brunswick green livery.

LMS 8F 2-8-0 No. 48151 has normally been based at Carnforth but did run some 'Cathedrals Express' trains in 2011. On 19 June it worked a train across London which unusually made a water stop at Wandsworth Town station. The hosepipe can be seen on the platform.

Southall is the London base for West Coast Railways where steam locomotives and the coaching stock are maintained. 8F 48151 and a pair of support coaches are seen at the station on 29 June 2011. The depot is to the right beyond the (now removed) footbridge.

'King' Class 6024 *King Edward I* passes Langley on the fast line with the 'Bristolian' to London, 3 March 2012.

Most steam workings from Waterloo these days are routed via the Windsor lines but here we have 'Black 5' No. 44932 passing Berrylands on the main line to Woking, 11 March 2012.

No. 71000 *Duke of Gloucester* heads for London Paddington at Langley on 6 June 2012 with the 'Diamond Jubilee Express'. Taken from the station footbridge, this train is on the slow lines and is about to pass through the platforms. Overhead electrification has since taken place on the GWR main line.

34067 *Tangmere* is running on the fast line as it runs south through Wandsworth Common station on 7 June 2012.

No. 70000 *Britannia* was now back in 'proper' BR lined green livery. It was seen near Hounslow on a cross-London 'Cathedrals Express' journey, 11 September 2012.

GWR 'Castle' 5043 *Earl of Mount Edgcumbe* heads a non-stop run on the fast line at Hanwell on 11 May 2013. Once again, the extra water carrier disguised as a full brake is behind the locomotive, which carries a replica of the GWR 'Cheltenham Flyer' headboard proclaiming it as 'The World's Fastest Train'.

For every steam excursion there is an accompanying empty stock move. 'Black 5' No. 44932 and its train are held at a signal check on the centre road at Kensington Olympia, while being towed south to take up a working the following day. Motive power is provided by West Coast Railways Class 47 No. 47580 *County of Essex*, which is in the livery applied by Stratford Depot for the Queen's Silver Jubilee in 1977. 15 June 2013.

Another repaint now sees 60163 *Tornado* in the dark blue livery applied by BR to some of the class when new. Taken at Harringay on 7 July 2013 working a 'Cathedrals Express'.

70013 *Oliver Cromwell* on 2 November 2013 with the first steam special through to the Bluebell Railway after it was linked to the National Rail network at East Grinstead. Here it waits at South Croydon station for a path on to the East Grinstead line, which branches off just south of here.

60009 *Union of South Africa* stands at the buffer stops at Kings Cross on 23 November 2013.

A pair of 'Black 5s' were provided for Steam Dream's pre-Christmas workings of 2013 and frequently these double-headed the trains. On this occasion 44871 and 45407 are in tandem passing Camden Road on 12 December 2013.

The North London line is the main route around the north side of London linking the lines out of each of the main termini. Despite an intensive ten-minute frequency passenger service by London Overground and several freight workings, paths are also found for steam excursions and their empty stock movements. Here 70000 *Britannia* is about to pass through Hampstead Heath on 15 March 2014 with a 'Cathedrals Express' heading westwards.

A stirring performance by 34046 *Braunton* as it storms through Harringay on 23 March 2014 with a 'Cathedrals Express'. Another locomotive rescued from Barry, this returned to the main line in 2013, its first run being on 14 August from Victoria to Weymouth.

Not all steam workings from London start at a terminus. On 26 April 2014 the 'Northern Belle' stock has arrived diesel-hauled at Hanwell loop sidings, where *Tangmere* has come from the nearby Southall Depot to take over the train for a trip to Kent. Here 34067 passes West Ealing near the beginning of its journey.

On the Catford loop 34067 *Tangmere* is all decked out with the 'Golden Arrow' regalia on a Pullman train for Canterbury, returning round the coast via Deal. Seen at Ravensbourne on 10 May 2014.

LMS Class 5 4-6-0 44932 approaches Olympia heading southwards on 29 May 2014.

A 'one-off' occurrence saw the restored GWR Railmotor No. 93 from the Didcot Steam Centre run trips over the now freight-only Brentford branch on 18 October 2014. These steam railmotors used to work over this line, amongst others, when new. The single-track line runs through a cutting, quite rural in appearance, such that its proximity to London is not apparent.

The most spectacular feature of the Brentford branch is here at Windmill Lane where three bridges carrying a road and the Grand Union Canal all cross the line at the same point.

A rare outing for 'Royal Scot' 46115 *Scots Guardsman* from St Pancras – one of the lesser-used stations for steam since its rebuilding to house Eurostar services. The loco passes through West Hampstead Midland with 'The Robin Hood' on 9 November 2014.

Originally saved by the B1 Locomotive Society in 1968, No. 61306 took the name *Mayflower* formerly carried by No. 61379. In 2014 it was purchased by David Buck, now the supremo of Steam Dreams, and returned to the main line in 2015. On 11 February 2015 it hauled 'The Royal Norfolkman' from Norwich to Windsor. The B1 is seen approaching Brentford station.

A few days later No. 61306 *Mayflower* was out again with a 'Cathedrals Express' and is seen on arrival back at Victoria on 14 February 2015.

A special evening train run on 4 June 2015 on behalf of the Railway Children charity whose aim is to protect street children. It was hauled by 35028 *Clan Line*, seen near Hounslow.

60163 *Tornado* threads through Putney on 8 August 2015, now back in apple green livery after its ventures in BR green and the BR blue.

The modern overhead electrification, installed through here originally for the Heathrow Connect service, doesn't manage to overwhelm the charm of the listed Brunel station at Hanwell as *Mayflower* passes through on 10 October 2015. This had just taken over the train at Hanwell sidings.

'Royal Scot' 46100 about to pass through Hanwell in the opposite direction with the Railway Touring Company's 'Great Britain IX' rail holiday tour, 24 April 2016.

The VSOE Orient Express Pullman coaches were now branded as the Belmond 'British Pullman' No. 34046 *Braunton* running as 34052 *Lord Dowding* approaches Staines with one of the regular Surrey Hills lunchtime circular services, 18 June 2016.

LMS 'Jubilee' 45699 *Galatea* with a special train for the Railway Touring Company at Putney, 9 July 2016 – a rare visit by this locomotive to the London area.

34046 *Braunton* running in the guise of long-gone 34052 *Lord Dowding* passes Shortlands on 24 July 2016. A West Coast Railways Class 37 diesel is tucked behind – perhaps because of fire risk?

60163 *Tornado* waits to depart from Kings Cross with the 'Magna Carta' tour, 8 October 2016.

46100 *Royal Scot* again works through the picturesque and listed GWR station at Hanwell, this time with a 'Cathedrals Express', 26 April 2017.

35028 *Clan Line* passes Mortlake 28 April 2017 'British Pullman'. While most 'Steam Dreams' tours westwards from Waterloo or Victoria take the Hounslow loop towards Staines, the 'British Pullman' is normally routed via Richmond.

Flying Scotsman was offered for sale by auction and secured for the nation by the National Railway Museum in 2004. However, its reliability was poor, and the resulting overhaul was to prove the most extensive and costly ever, taking ten years and over £3m. Finally, it was back on the main line, this time in BR green as No. 60103, which is the most appropriate for its condition with double chimney and smoke deflectors. It was seen here at the starting point for many of London's steam specials, Victoria's platform 2, on 3 June 2017.

60103 *Flying Scotsman* at South Acton on 15 September 2017 with a 'Cathedrals Express' on the spur from Kew West Junction to the North London line. The lines turning off to the left lead to Richmond and are served by London Overground trains from Stratford.

The 'Belmond British Pullman' is normally the preserve of *Clan Line*, but when that is unavailable other locomotives may be deployed. On 1 July 2017, unusually, it was 46100 *Royal Scot* and this was photographed approaching East Croydon on the return leg of the round trip.

35028 *Clan Line* heads down the main line at Raynes Park with the 'Waterloo Sunset' on 9 July 2017. A train is run each year as close as possible to the day when steam ended on the Southern Region with the electrification through to Bournemouth on 9 July 1967, so this marked fifty years to the day.

'Black 5' 45212 takes the Hounslow loop and approaches Brentford on 15 May 2018.

On 24 November 2018 *Clan Line* worked a tour from Paddington which was routed via the old GWR Birmingham main line route to West Ruislip. This line, coming off at Old Oak Common, was severed shortly afterwards in connection with work for HS2, making this the last steam working over this route. In less-than-ideal weather 35028 passes Park Royal. To the left is the site of the former spur to the Guinness factory.

Steam Dreams continue to run a number of trips in the run-up to Christmas and on 21 December 'Black 5' No. 44871 was employed on a journey to Canterbury. Photographed approaching Swanley station, Christmas tinsel has been wrapped around the handrails and the smokebox door handle.

2019 was the twentieth anniversary year for Steam Dreams. The programme included trips hauled by *Flying Scotsman*. Here the A3 is seen just west of Putney station on 1 June – the destination was Salisbury.

'Black 5' 44871 speeds through Hanwell with a Steam Dreams journey from London Paddington to Bath and Bristol. The period look of this delightful listed station is beginning to be spoilt as it prepares for the (late) arrival of Crossrail. Note the bracket arms for the CCTV cameras needed for one-person operation. Above the Up side station building can be seen scaffolding as lifts to the subway are being installed to allow step-free accessibility. 20 June 2019.

On 4 June, the first day of the 'Royal Windsor Steam Express', 61306 *Mayflower* on the second departure from Waterloo approaches Brentford. This engine had been out of action for three years after boiler problems experienced at the end of 2015 proved more serious than expected and led to a full general overhaul.

· THE ·
ROYAL WINDSOR
STEAM EXPRESS
TRAVEL FROM LONDON TO
WINDSOR BY STEAM TRAIN
Fares from £35
CALL
01483 209888
VISIT
RoyalWindsorSteamExpress.co.uk

· THE ·
SUNSET
STEAM EXPRESS
STEAM TRAIN DINING
FROM LONDON
Nº 61306
Dining Fares from £99
CALL
01483 209888
VISIT
SunsetSteamExpress.co.uk

On 25 June the 'Black 5' was employed on the 'Royal Windsor Steam Express' rather than the advertised B1. Here it is on the 11.10 departure from Waterloo nearing Brentford. Later 44871 would be sent to Scotland for the summer 'Jacobite' workings.

The B1 worked the remainder of the 'Royal Windsor Steam Express' trips and here it storms through Kensington Olympia on 20 August with the first journey of the day, the 8.00 a.m. from Waterloo which was routed via Kensington Olympia and the Kew West curve rather than via Clapham Junction.

Approaching the end of its journey, 61306 crosses the river and slows to enter Windsor & Eton Riverside station on 27 August, the last Tuesday of the 2019 season. Following the success of these trains there were due to be additional trains on Fridays or Saturdays between June and September for the 2020 season. However, trains will depart from Victoria rather than Waterloo.

If the Windsor trains and evening dining train via Guildford were not enough, *Mayflower* was out again on Thursday 4 July when it was used on a Steam Dreams excursion from Liverpool Street to Norwich and Dereham, on the Mid-Norfolk Railway. On a very hot and sunny day the train ascends Brentwood bank. A West Coast Railways Class 33 diesel was on the back of the train. This was the first steam working out of Liverpool Street station in 2019, on a line where B1s would have been regular performers in the past.

A very different day on 18 July which dawned with heavy cloud and showers. *Mayflower* worked a Steam Dreams excursion starting from Southend East and destined for Winchester and Eastleigh. Here the B1 is seen in a very urban setting, departing from Stratford and passing Lea Junction as it heads round the North London line. The engine is crossing the River Lea. To the right beyond the construction work is the Queen Elizabeth Olympic Park, and the skyline is dominated by the Westfield Shopping Centre.

Back on old familiar territory for Steam Dreams. On 19 September 2019 *Mayflower* passes through Peckham Rye on a trip to Faversham via the Kent coast and Canterbury.

Bibliography

Harris, Nigel, *Steam All the Way* (St Michael's on Wyre: Silver Link, 1987)

Jackson, Joan, *Steam Returns to London* (Shepperton: Ian Allan, 1990)

Kennedy, Rex, *Ian Allan's 50 Years of Railways 1942-1992* (London: BCA/Ian Allan, 1992)

Morrison, Gavin, *Britain's Railways 1948-1998: A Personal View of 50 Years of Change* (Shepperton: Ian Allan, 1999)

Nixon, L. A., *A Decade of Steam Running 1971-1981* (Shepperton: Ian Allan, 1981)

Sharman, Bill, *Main Line Steam: 25 Glorious Years of Preservation* (Penrhyn: Atlantic, 1997)

Sharpe, Brian, *LNER Steam Revival* (Horncastle: Mortons, 2014)

Sharpe, Brian, Southern Steam Revival (Horncastle: Mortons, 2014)

Various magazines including *Heritage Railway*, *Railway Magazine* and *Steam Railway*